W9-AOE-353

MAR 2 4 2009

BILLY the KID

REVISED EDITION

WANTED
DEAD OR ALIVE

By Carl R. Green and William R. Sanford

E **Enslow Publishers, Inc.**

40 Industrial Road
Box 398
Berkeley Heights, NJ 07922
USA

http://www.enslow.com

Original edition published in 1992.

Library of Congress Cataloging-in-Publication Data
Green, Carl R.
 Billy the Kid / Carl R. Green and William R. Sanford. — Rev. ed.
  p. cm. — (Outlaws and lawmen of the wild West)
 Summary: "Readers will find out about the life and death of Billy the Kid"—Provided by publisher.
 Includes bibliographical references and index.
 ISBN 978-0-7660-3173-9
 1. Billy, the Kid—Juvenile literature. 2. Outlaws—Southwest, New—Biography—Juvenile literature. 3. Southwest, New—Biography—Juvenile literature. I. Sanford, William R. (William Reynolds), 1927– II. Title.
 F786.B54G743 2009
 364.15'52092—dc22
 [B]
                        2008010006

ISBN-10: 0-7660-3173-X

Printed in the United States of America

10 9 8 7 6 5 4 3 2 1

To Our Readers:
We have done our best to make sure all Internet Addresses in this book were active and appropriate when we went to press. However, the authors and the publisher have no control over and assume no liability for the material available on those Internet sites or on other Web sites they may link to. Any comments or suggestions can be sent by e-mail to comments@enslow.com or to the address on the back cover.

♻ Enslow Publishers, Inc., is committed to printing our books on recycled paper. The paper in every book contains 10% to 30% post-consumer waste (PCW). The cover board on the outside of each book contains 100% PCW. Our goal is to do our part to help young people and the environment too!

Interior photos: Alamy/Photos 12, p. 21; Alamy/M. L. Pearson, p. 38; Alamy/Danita Delimont, p. 41; Alamy/Don Despain/www.rekindlephotos.com, p. 43; AP Photo/Museum of New Mexico, Napoleon Sarony, p. 29; The Bridgeman Art Library/Private Collection, Peter Newark Western Americana, pp. 11, 32; Getty Images/MPI, pp. 15, 40; Getty Images/Peter Stackpole/Time Life Pictures, p. 17; The Granger Collection, New York, pp. 1, 9, 27, 33, 36; iStockphoto/spxChrome, (marshal badge), odd pages; iStockphoto/Alex Bramwell (revolver), even pages; iStockphoto/billnoll (frame), p. 4; iStockphoto/GaryAlvis, p. 26; The Kobal Collection/20th Century Fox, p. 44; Legends of America, pp. 5, 19; Library of Congress, pp. 7, 24, 30; Museum of New Mexico, p. 6; U.S. National Archives, p. 12; Courtesy of the National Parks Service, p. 23; Shutterstock/Dhoxax (background), pp. 3, 5, 8–9, 14–15, 20–21, 27, 35, 42–43.

Cover photo: The Granger Collection, New York (*The outlaw who became famous as Billy the Kid was known by several names throughout his life. He was born Henry McCarty in 1859.*)

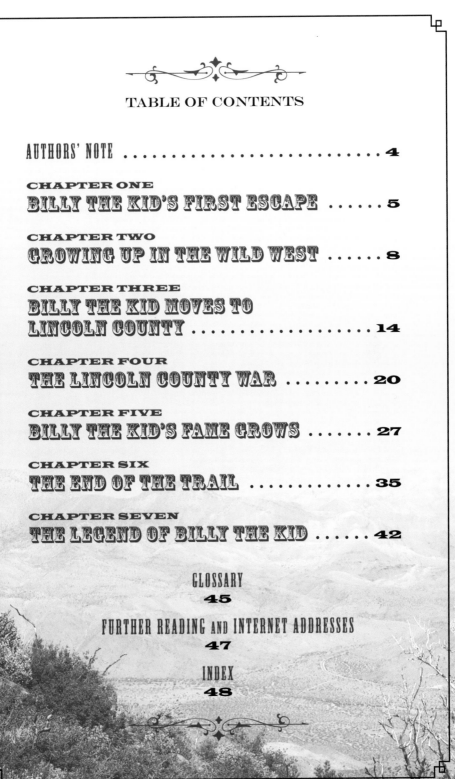

TABLE OF CONTENTS

··· A U T H O R S' N O T E ···

This book tells the true story of the western

outlaw known as Billy the Kid. The Kid was as

well known in the 1880s as pop stars are

today. People all over the country talked

about the exploits of this fiery young outlaw.

To satisfy the demand, newspapers rushed

into print with stories about his life and his

crimes. Thus, the stories and quotes used in

this book all are drawn from firsthand reports.

CHAPTER ONE

BILLY THE KID'S FIRST ESCAPE

In 1875, Henry Antrim was a fifteen-year-old teenager. He was living in Silver City, New Mexico. His mother was dead, and he had been taken in by Mrs. Sarah Brown and her family. Henry was small for his age. No one could have guessed that history would remember him as the outlaw Billy the Kid.

Even in those days, Henry was no angel. To raise some cash he stole a tub of butter and sold it to a Silver City store. When the crime

Even as a youngster, Henry Antrim was well on his way to becoming the famous outlaw known as Billy the Kid.

Billy the Kid's hometown of Silver City, New Mexico, was just one of many small, rough towns that flourished in the Wild West.

was reported, the local sheriff tracked him down. To punish the boy, the sheriff turned Henry over his knee and gave him a spanking.

The spanking had little effect. As he would do all his life, Henry chose the wrong kind of friends. One buddy was a thief called Sombrero Jack. Jack took some clothes from a Chinese laundry and gave them to Henry to hide at Mrs. Brown's house. When Mrs. Brown found the bundle, she called the sheriff.

Sombrero Jack ran off, leaving Henry to take the blame. This time, the sheriff punished the boy more harshly. He dragged Henry off to jail.

Because he was so young, Henry was not locked in a cell. The sheriff gave him a bed in a hallway instead. If Henry had served his time, he soon would have been set free. Instead, he waited until the sheriff went to lunch. Then he escaped by climbing up the chimney. Once he was free, Henry quickly put Silver City behind him.

Four years passed before Henry Antrim became known as Billy the Kid. His life as an outlaw, however, had already begun.

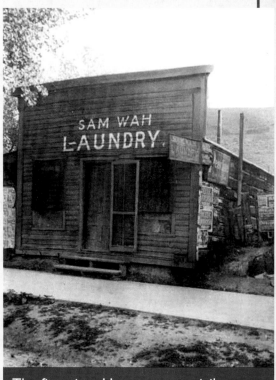

The first time Henry went to jail, it was for stealing from a Chinese laundry similar to this one in Colorado City, Colorado. After escaping, he took up the outlaw life.

CHAPTER TWO

GROWING UP IN THE WILD WEST

Western writers agree that Billy the Kid was born in New York City. Catherine McCarty, his mother, named him Henry. Born in Ireland, Catherine came to America to escape a famine. She also gave birth to a second son, Joe. Beyond these facts, writers often differ in their stories.

When was Henry born? The records show he was most likely born on November 23, 1859. What happened to his father? He may have died when the boy was very young. Some say he was murdered. Was Joe older or younger than Henry? No one knows.

Henry's life is easier to trace after Catherine moved west with her sons. In Minnesota, she met William Antrim. The two fell in love, but they did not marry right away. They moved to Wichita, Kansas, where Catherine washed clothes for a living. She was a hard worker and her laundry business did well until

When Catherine and William Antrim moved their family to Silver City, New Mexico, in 1873, they settled in a log cabin near a stream. This illustration from 1871 shows a typical cabin in the West.

she fell ill. A doctor examined her and said her lungs were diseased. There was only one treatment. She had to move to a high, dry climate.

Catherine and William took the boys to Santa Fe, New Mexico. The couple married there in 1873. From Santa Fe, the family's search for a healthy climate led them to Silver City. This mountain mining town lies in the southwest corner of New Mexico.

The Antrims lived in a log cabin near a stream. William worked at odd jobs when he was not prospecting for gold. Catherine took in boarders to help pay the bills. Young Henry watched his mother grow weaker and weaker. At last the time came when she could no longer leave her bed. Catherine died in 1874.

Henry was still a schoolboy when he lost his mother. The small, thin boy had been a good student. Now, with his mother dead, schoolwork no longer appealed to him. He also found it hard to get along with his stepfather. Henry solved the problem by quitting school and moving in with the Browns. He paid for his keep by working in a butcher shop. In later years, the people of Silver City recalled Henry's love of music and dancing. He even took part in a show held at the opera house.

Growing up in Silver City left its mark on Henry. Life on the frontier was violent. The men carried guns, and many were quick to use them. Some gambled and drank too much. Henry began to believe that only fools worked hard for money. It seemed easier to take what one wanted, no matter what the law said.

Henry also learned the "Code of the West." One of the rules was that all wrongs must be avenged. To do nothing in the face of an insult was the coward's way. When Henry escaped from the Silver City jail

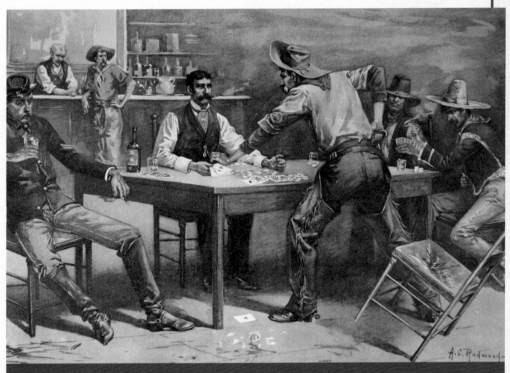

Growing up in the Wild West left its mark on the boy who became Billy the Kid. He saw that most men carried guns, and were quick to use them to settle their disputes.

he was only fifteen. Even so, he was learning to take care of himself.

Henry headed west to Arizona after he left Silver City. There he found a job on a ranch near Camp Grant. A town boy all his life, Henry had never learned the skills a cowboy needs. He had to learn how to ride a horse, rope a cow, and fire a gun. He learned quickly, but he was a boy trying to do a man's job. The ranch foreman fired him.

In 1876, Henry joined a gang of small-time thieves. His best friend in the gang was John Mackie. The older man had a long history of lawbreaking. He and Henry began by stealing saddles and blankets. Growing bolder, they moved up to stealing horses. After each theft, they rode to far-off ranches and sold the stolen animals.

Henry soon picked the wrong man to rob. After the young outlaw stole his horse, Sergeant Lewis Hartman and four friends tracked Henry northward. They caught up with the thief near Globe City, Arizona. Hartman took back his horse and left Henry on foot. A few months later, Hartman filed a complaint with the sheriff. Henry ended up in jail.

Henry hated being locked up. One day he threw salt in a guard's eyes and tried to escape. The other

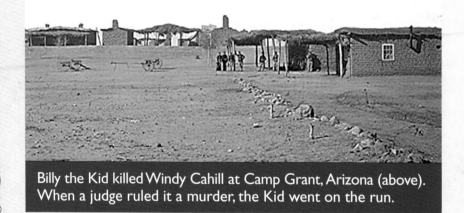

Billy the Kid killed Windy Cahill at Camp Grant, Arizona (above). When a judge ruled it a murder, the Kid went on the run.

guards caught him and shackled his legs with iron chains. Henry escaped again that night, chains and all. In the weeks that followed, he was caught twice more—and escaped each time.

Slowly, the trouble died down. By the summer of 1877, Henry had drifted back to Camp Grant. People now called him "Kid" because he looked so young. Despite his looks, the Kid was far from childlike. He carried a pistol stuffed under his belt.

The Kid was quick to laugh and most people liked him. Windy Cahill, however, liked to bully him. The big blacksmith thought it was fun to slap the Kid and knock him down. One day, the two called each other a few bad names too many. That started a real fight. As they wrestled, the heavier Cahill pinned the Kid to the floor. With his free hand, the Kid yanked out his pistol. The gun roared and Cahill fell back, shot in the stomach. The blacksmith died the next day.

A jury ruled that the shooting was murder. The Kid did not wait to be put in jail. He rode east to New Mexico and holed up on a ranch near Silver City. The ranchers fed their guest and gave him a bed. With the law on his trail, the Kid could not relax. Two weeks later, he took to the road again.

CHAPTER THREE

BILLY THE KID MOVES TO LINCOLN COUNTY

Henry "Kid" Antrim was growing up. When he first left Silver City he was a small-time thief. Now, two years later, he was a horse thief and a cattle rustler. He had killed his first man. When he had money, he went to saloons to dance and play cards. Unlike most of his friends, he did not smoke or drink.

At seventeen, the Kid was a slim, wiry young man. He weighed 135 pounds and looked taller than his five feet, eight inches. His hair was light brown, and his eyes were blue. When he smiled, his two front teeth stuck out. That ready smile made it easy to attract girls. His Mexican girlfriends also liked his blue eyes and good Spanish.

Some writers tell us that the Kid dressed like a movie cowboy. They describe his "buckskin pants with gold bells sewed to the sides." His hat, they say, sparkled with gold and jewels. The stories make good reading, but they are pure fiction. The Kid dressed simply. He wore a dark coat and pants, a vest, and polished boots. His hat was a Mexican sombrero with a green band.

Even though he was an outlaw, the Kid was easy to like. He was generous, brave, and full of fun. Unlike many cowboys, he could read and write. His friends knew he could be counted on. When he was in a tight spot, he often cracked a joke. His good humor, however, hid a fierce temper. When he was angry, he often acted without thinking. This trait sometimes led him into serious trouble.

Henry "Kid" Antrim may have been a rough character, but he was well-liked and had many friends.

After leaving the ranch near Silver City, the Kid joined a gang of rustlers. Jesse Evans led the gang from its base at Mesilla, New Mexico. They stole horses and cattle in New Mexico and in Texas. They even crossed the border into Mexico to steal cattle. Life with the Evans gang rounded out the Kid's training as an outlaw. He became a crack shot with both pistol and rifle.

In September 1877, the gang stole three horses from a camp in the Burro Mountains. After the owners tracked the thieves for a time, they returned to Mesilla. Kid Antrim, they told the sheriff, was part of the gang. The local paper printed the story. Once again, the Kid and his friends were wanted men.

With the law hot on their trail, the gang broke up. The Kid still worried that he might be jailed for shooting Windy Cahill. Friends told him to hide in Mexico. Instead, he chose to rejoin Jesse Evans. By this time Evans had led the rest of the gang to New Mexico's Lincoln County. The county was a hard three-day ride from Arizona. That seemed far enough to be safe.

The Kid did not look like a gunslinger when he reached Lincoln County. After Apache Indians stole his horse, he walked for miles to reach a ranch house. The rancher's wife fed him and nursed his bloody feet. When the Kid left, she loaned him a horse.

The Kid was now calling himself Billy Bonney. He again hooked up with Jesse Evans and his gang. In a short time, the gang's livestock thefts were the talk of

In late 1877, Billy the Kid moved on to Lincoln, New Mexico. Jimmy Dolan's general store (above), was the town's only two-story building.

Lincoln County. Sheriff Brady arrested Evans and three of his men. The "jail" was a hole in the ground topped with a log guardroom. The Kid and the rest of the gang promptly rescued their friends. Most of the outlaws fled, but the Kid stayed behind.

The town of Lincoln was the center of county life. Four hundred people lived there. A mile of mud-brick buildings lined a shady street. The town's only two-story building housed a general store. Another building served as courtroom and dance hall.

Jimmy Dolan, who owned the general store, ruled Lincoln County. Dolan and his friends made money any way they could. They bought stolen cattle from the Evans gang for five dollars a head. Then they sold it to the army for fifteen dollars a head.

The town was growing. Men moved in who did not like the way Jimmy Dolan ran things. Rancher John Tunstall took the lead in fighting back. With the help of a lawyer named Alexander McSween, Tunstall opened a second general store. As Dolan's profits fell, he tried to scare Tunstall into leaving. Tunstall told his foreman to hire some gunmen for protection.

The foreman chose the Kid to work on the ranch. Tunstall liked the Kid and treated him fairly. The Kid repaid the rancher with his loyalty. If there was shooting, the Kid vowed, he would fight for his new friend.

The Kid did not have long to wait. Lawyer McSween had been hired to collect $47,000 for one of Dolan's friends. McSween did so, but he kept the money. Some of it was owed to him, and he said he was not sure who should get the rest. That was too much for Dolan's friend. He charged the lawyer with breaking the law. A friendly judge signed an order that tied up all of McSween's money.

Dolan knew that McSween owned half of Tunstall's store. With Sheriff Brady's backing, Dolan took over the store. The loss of their business added more fuel to Tunstall and McSween's anger. The

Jimmy Dolan was the "boss" of Lincoln County. When some newcomers tried to end his reign, a serious conflict erupted.

rancher told his men to ride with their guns loaded. Lincoln County was about to go to war.

CHAPTER FOUR

THE LINCOLN COUNTY WAR

A few days passed. The shooting started when Sheriff Brady sent a posse to the Tunstall ranch. Brady's orders were based on a legal paper that claimed some of the ranch's horses belonged to McSween. His men had orders to round up those horses and deliver them to Dolan.

The posse met Tunstall, the Kid, and three cowboys near the ranch. The Kid and the cowboys sensed danger and took cover. Tunstall made the fatal mistake of staying to talk. As the posse approached, a deputy pulled his gun and killed him.

The killing touched off a shooting war. Sheriff Brady, the district judge, and the Evans gang backed Dolan. The town constable and the justice of the peace sided with McSween. Tunstall's crew formed a

The 1973 film *Pat Garrett and Billy the Kid* is just one of several movies that have been made about the Kid's life. It starred Kris Kristofferson (above) as Billy the Kid.

posse of gunmen who also took McSween's side. The Kid joined this bunch, who called themselves the Regulators. He was eager to avenge his friend's death.

Most of Lincoln County was pulling for McSween. Two bloody events, however, changed people's minds. First, the Regulators tracked down two men from the posse that had killed Tunstall. The men gave up, thinking they would be taken back to town. They guessed wrong. The Kid and one of his buddies shot both of them.

Next, the Regulators plotted to kill Sheriff Brady. The Kid and five other men hid behind the general store one night. They opened fire when Brady and two deputies left the courthouse the next morning. The shots killed Brady and one deputy. When the Kid ran out to grab Brady's rifle, the second deputy shot him in the leg. Somehow, the Kid managed to drag himself to safety. His friends in town hid him while the wound healed.

A grand jury charged that both sides were to blame for the killings. The charges did not settle the feud, however. A new gunfight broke out in April. A troop of U.S. Army soldiers had to be called in to separate the warring factions.

The last battle began on June 14, 1878. That night, McSween led sixty Regulators into Lincoln. Working fast, they turned two stores and the McSween home into forts. The new sheriff and his posse dug in to face the invaders. For three days, the two sides fired at anything that moved. Neither side would back down.

Word of the renewed fighting reached the army. Soldiers led by Colonel Nathan Dudley moved in with their cannon. Colonel Dudley, it turned out, favored the Dolan side. He ordered his gunners to aim at

McSween's makeshift forts. Many of the Regulators ran away when they saw the heavy guns pointed at them.

McSween held out in his house until the sheriff's men set it on fire. Choking from the smoke, the Kid told the men who were left to run for the river. Everyone but McSween escaped. He was dressed in a white shirt, and was an easy target. A burst of gunfire cut him down.

Colonel Nathan Dudley and his troops were called in to put an end to the violence in Lincoln.

With McSween dead, the Lincoln County War was over. Neither side could say it had won. Without a leader, many of the Regulators drifted away. For his part, Dolan had run out of cash.

The Mescalero Apache Agency trading post, where the Kid ran into still more trouble, probably looked much like this Wild West trading post.

The Kid stayed in Lincoln to be near his friends. The gang of ex-Regulators kept things stirred up. They stole horses and made threats against Dolan. Loyal to the Code of the West, they wanted revenge for the deaths of their friends.

In August 1878, the Kid stumbled into more trouble. At the time he was riding with the gang near the Mescalero Apache Agency trading post. The Kid and half of the gang stopped to drink at a spring. The others rode on toward the post. All at once, some Indians opened fire on the riders. Inside the post, the agency chief and his clerk heard the shots. The two men thought the gang was coming to kill them. They tried to flee, only to run into the angry gang members. Guns roared and the clerk fell dead. The agency chief retreated to the trading post.

Out at the spring, the gunfire spooked the horses. The Kid's horse ran off, leaving him on foot. Ducking as bullets zipped near his head, the Kid jumped onto George Coe's horse. With the Kid riding double, Coe and the others circled the agency. The Kid caught a pony in the agency corral and rode it bareback to the gang's hideout.

News of the shoot-out spread quickly. Everyone blamed the Kid for the clerk's death. Colonel Dudley sent soldiers to arrest him. The soldiers came back empty-handed. The Kid and his friends had already left the county.

A week later, the Kid turned up at the ranch of John Chisum. Chisum had been Tunstall's friend and owned a large spread. Sallie Chisum, the owner's niece, was said to be one of the Kid's sweethearts. The Chisums were about to drive their cattle north to Fort Sumner. The Kid joined them.

At Fort Sumner, the Kid spent his nights dancing with the local girls. Restless as always, he still wanted

The Kid was on the trail, driving some stolen horses to Texas, when he decided it was time to end the Lincoln County War.

revenge for the events in Lincoln. He put out the word that the surviving members of the old gang should join him.

In late September, the revived gang stole some horses and drove them to Texas. The ranchers there bought the horses, no questions asked. The Kid stayed in Texas for a month. Then he headed back toward Lincoln. One by one, his gang drifted off. Only his best friend, Tom O'Folliard, was left to ride with him.

During that long trail ride, the Kid had a change of heart. He said he was no longer thirsting for revenge. For once, Billy the Kid was ready to make peace.

... C H A P T E R   F I V E ...

BILLY THE KID'S FAME GROWS

It was now 1879, one year after Tunstall's death. The Kid said he was ready to talk about ending the shooting. Jimmy Dolan's friends agreed to meet him in Lincoln.

Twenty men met in the middle of the main street. Gang leader Jesse Evans screamed that the Kid could not be trusted. He said they should kill him right there. The Kid kept the peace by pledging that he was not there to fight. Calmer now, the two sides agreed to end the killing. They also promised not to testify in court about the case. If someone did, the others vowed to kill him. After the terms were written down, they all signed the paper.

In 1879 the Kid was ready to call a truce in the Lincoln County War. Despite his resolve, the shooting continued.

The two gangs went to a saloon to celebrate. The Kid was one of the few who stayed sober. When they left the saloon, the Kid, Dolan, and the other outlaws met lawyer Huston Chapman. Chapman had been hired to bring legal charges against McSween's killers. Dolan and his friends hated him.

A Dolan man named Bill Campbell pulled a pistol. Pointing it at Chapman, he ordered the lawyer to dance for him. Chapman refused. Blind with rage, Dolan fired his own pistol into the ground. Startled by the shot, Campbell pulled the trigger. Chapman fell with a bullet in his chest. His killers left him there and moved on to a second saloon.

Word of the murder brought the governor to Lincoln. Lew Wallace had been a Civil War general. In later years, he won fame as the author of the novel *Ben Hur.* For the moment, his job was to end the shooting. As a first step, Wallace offered a pardon to those who had not been indicted by a grand jury. That did not help the Kid. He had already been indicted for two killings.

In March 1880, the Kid wrote to Governor Wallace to ask for a meeting. He said he would testify about the Chapman murder. Doing so would break his promise to Dolan, but the Kid badly wanted a pardon. Wallace agreed to meet with him.

The Kid gave himself up a week later. Wallace placed him under guard in the house next door to his own. The Kid met with the governor and described his life as an outlaw. Wallace listened, but went back to Santa Fe without granting the pardon.

The grand jury met in April. Many of its members were McSween's friends. The Kid named Dolan and Campbell as Chapman's killers. The jury, in turn, indicted the two men for murder. It also indicted Colonel Dudley for burning the McSween house.

The Kid stayed to serve as a witness, but Campbell fled the county.

Lew Wallace was a former Civil War general and the governor of New Mexico. The Kid hoped Wallace would pardon him, but the governor never did.

When the two cases went to trial, the juries refused to convict Dolan. At that point the district attorney pulled a double cross. He filed papers to put the Kid on trial for the murder of Sheriff Brady.

Because he was expecting a pardon, the Kid felt betrayed. He climbed on his horse and rode out of Lincoln. Some townsfolk claimed that the new sheriff looked the other way. If so, he must have agreed that the Kid had been treated badly.

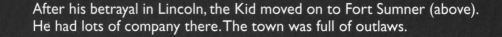

After his betrayal in Lincoln, the Kid moved on to Fort Sumner (above). He had lots of company there. The town was full of outlaws.

The Kid moved on to Fort Sumner. The small town was a hundred miles northeast of Lincoln. Although he was a wanted man, he was welcome there. Mexican sheepherders gave him a place to sleep. Some of the local girls fell for his boyish good looks.

To keep busy, the Kid dealt cards in the saloons. He also had a good time at the town's weekly dances.

Fort Sumner was a meeting place for outlaws that summer. A number of them had been driven west by the Texas state police. Others came in on the Santa Fe railroad. The kid teamed up with some of his old gang. Once more they rode the range, stealing horses and cattle.

The legend of Billy the Kid added a new chapter that summer. A cowboy named Joe Grant had been bragging that he was going to kill the Kid. Grant was drunk when he followed the Kid into a saloon one night. Thinking fast, the Kid pulled Grant's gun from its holster. While he pretended to admire the weapon, he turned the cylinder. Then he gave the gun back to the drunken bully. Now, if Grant pulled the trigger, the hammer would fall on an empty chamber.

Grant, spoiling for a fight, threatened to shoot one of the Kid's friends. The Kid laughed and told him he was aiming at the wrong man. Grant called him a liar. The Kid shrugged and walked away. Grant raised his gun and aimed at the Kid's back. When he pulled the trigger the hammer clicked on the empty chamber. Hearing the click, the Kid drew his own gun. Spinning around, he drilled Grant with three quick shots.

Not long after that, the Kid went to see John Chisum. He complained that Chisum had not paid him for his work in Lincoln County. Chisum laughed and told the Kid he had been paid fairly. The Kid was angry, but he did not want to shoot the old man. With the help of his gang, he drove off some of Chisum's cattle instead.

Almost every ranch was losing cattle to rustlers. The ranchers needed a strong sheriff who would protect their herds. John Chisum's choice was the

With so many outlaws in Fort Sumner, it was no wonder that the local ranchers (above) lost so many cattle. The Kid, never one to pass up an easy dollar, joined his rustler friends in raiding the herds.

six-foot, six-inch Pat Garrett. Garrett was new to the job, but he was honest, smart, and tough. The former bartender also knew Billy the Kid's hiding places. At first, Garrett served as a deputy sheriff. He was well liked, and he became the Lincoln County sheriff on January 1, 1881.

All this time, the Kid's fame as a gunslinger was growing. If a crime took place in New Mexico, Billy the Kid was said to be behind it. One story said he was passing fake

Pat Garrett became the new Lincoln County sheriff in 1881. One of his main goals was to capture Billy the Kid.

money. Another claimed that he was robbing the U.S. mails. At one point the Kid's gang did steal sixteen horses. A posse trailed the horse thieves to a house near White Oaks. A member of the posse named Jimmy Carlyle went in to talk the gang into giving up. Someone in the house pulled a gun and killed the unarmed man. After a long standoff, the posse gave up and rode off. The Kid and his gang mounted up and vanished into the night.

The press reported that Billy the Kid had shot Carlyle. It was the first time his nickname was seen in print. The news of the killing angered Governor Wallace. He put up a large reward for the Kid's capture.

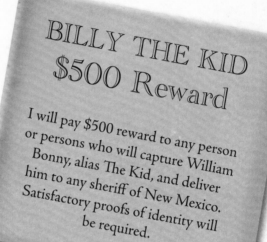

BILLY THE KID
$500 Reward

I will pay $500 reward to any person or persons who will capture William Bonny, alias The Kid, and deliver him to any sheriff of New Mexico. Satisfactory proofs of identity will be required.

By 1880 the Kid had a long list of crimes on his record. To speed up the hunt for the elusive young outlaw, Nevada's governor put this reward notice in the *Las Vegas Gazette*. Notice that the name "Bonney" was not spelled correctly.

CHAPTER SIX

THE END OF THE TRAIL

The Kid returned to Fort Sumner as winter closed in. He visited friends, went to dances, and slept in an empty building.

Pat Garrett heard that the Kid had returned. Seeing a chance to catch the young outlaw, he led a posse to Fort Sumner. He rode into town on December 17, 1880, but he was too late. The Kid had vanished. Would he come back? Garrett waited around to see.

The Kid and his gang returned during a snowstorm. Perhaps the Kid sensed that Garrett and his posse were lying in wait. At the last minute, he moved to the back of the line of riders. The posse opened fire as the outlaws rode into the trap. Tom O'Folliard was killed, but the Kid and the others escaped.

The posse tracked the outlaws to a stone hut near Stinking Springs. At first light, Garrett saw one of the gang members standing in the doorway. Rifles cracked.

This illustration shows Billy the Kid shooting a drifter who had pointed a gun at him. The Kid's violent ways finally caught up with him when he was sentenced to hang in April 1881. However, he managed to escape once again.

The man fell back into the tiny hut. A minute later he staggered out, his hands in the air. Badly wounded, he died an hour later.

The Kid's only hope was to escape on horseback. He tried to pull a horse into the hut, but Garrett shot it. The dead horse now blocked the only way out. Garrett called to the Kid to give himself up. The Kid yelled back, "Come and get me!"

The outlaws were tough, brave men—but they were running out of food. The smell of the posse's cooking fires made their mouths water. At last the Kid and the others came out with their hands raised.

Garrett took his captives to a jail in Las Vegas. Despite his arrest, the Kid was cheerful enough. He talked with a reporter while he tried on a new suit, a gift from a friend. The Kid liked the suit, but he thought the jail was second rate. "Is the jail at Santa Fe any better than this?" he asked.

Before long, the Kid got his answer. He was taken to the Santa Fe jail, where he spent the next three months. From there, he wrote to Governor Wallace to ask about his long-delayed pardon. Wallace did not reply. In March, the Kid was sent to Mesilla, New Mexico, and put on trial. The trial lasted just one day. On April 13, 1881, the judge sentenced the Kid to be hanged.

Garrett moved the Kid to the Lincoln County courthouse. To prevent an escape attempt, he bound the Kid with handcuffs and leg irons. Bob Olinger and James Bell were ordered to guard the prisoner. Olinger cruelly cursed the Kid and hit him when no one was looking.

The Kid's chance to escape came on April 28. Garrett left to buy lumber for the scaffold on which the Kid would be hanged. With Olinger away on an errand, the Kid asked Bell to take him to the outdoor toilet. He found a gun there, hidden by a friend. On the way back, he slipped one wrist out of the handcuffs. Bell tried to run, but he was not quick enough. The Kid shot him in the back. Then the Kid picked up a shotgun and waited. When Olinger returned, he shot him, too.

J. W. BELL
DIED HERE
KILLED BY BILLY THE KID
APRIL 28, 1881

Markers placed near the Lincoln County courthouse commemorate the deaths of James Bell (above) and Bob Olinger.

Next, the Kid used a pickax to break one of the leg irons. With the chain tucked into his belt, he climbed on a horse and rode away. No one tried to stop him.

The Kid did not go far after he left Lincoln. He rode to a nearby house where a friend cut off his chains. Another friend gave him a horse and urged him to flee to Mexico. The Kid shook his head. He said he would go back to Fort Sumner instead.

Nine days later, the Kid slipped into Fort Sumner. This time he was more careful. He slept at farms and sheep camps. At night, he sneaked into town to go to dances. On other nights he visited his sweethearts.

The Las Vegas paper reported that the Kid was in Fort Sumner. The news amazed Sheriff Garrett.

He thought his quarry would be far away by now. Three months after the Kid's escape, Garrett saddled up a three-man posse.

Garrett and his men reached Fort Sumner on July 14, 1881. They had to stay out of sight because the Kid had friends in town. That night the lawmen set a trap, hoping the Kid would walk into it. They did not see their quarry slip into Celsa Gutiérrez's house. Celsa was one of the Kid's girlfriends.

The lawmen talked it over. Were they wasting their time? Garrett said he would talk to his old friend Pete Maxwell. Maxwell, he thought, might tell them where to find the Kid. His men stayed outside while Garrett went into Maxwell's bedroom to wake him up. It was nearly midnight.

Back at Celsa's house, the Kid said he was hungry. He knew that Pete Maxwell had a side of meat hanging on his porch. Still in his stocking feet, he headed for Maxwell's house. Knife in hand, he was ready to carve himself a steak.

The Kid almost bumped into Garrett's men. Springing back, he drew his pistol. In a whisper he said, "¿Quién es?" (Spanish for "Who are you?") The men did not know the stranger was Billy the Kid. One of them told him not to be afraid.

This drawing of Billy's shoot-out with Pat Garrett was printed in a dime novel. The Kid is at left, and Garrett is the second shooter.

By now Maxwell was wide awake. He told Garrett that the Kid was staying at a sheep ranch near town. Then the two men heard the voices outside. A moment later, someone entered the darkened room.

"Who are those fellows outside, Pete?" a voice asked.

Maxwell sat up and yelled, "That's him!"

The Kid now saw a second shadowy figure in the bedroom.

"¿Quién es? ¿Quién es?" he demanded.

Garrett knew that voice. He drew his pistol and fired twice. The first bullet struck the Kid just above the heart. He died instantly.

The shots brought people running from nearby houses. Some of the townsfolk cursed Garrett for killing the Kid. The sheriff and his men had to stay on guard all that night. They had good reason to fear an attack by the Kid's friends.

A jury later ruled that Garrett shot the Kid in the line of duty. On July 15, 1881, Billy the Kid was buried at Fort Sumner. The young gunslinger was only twenty-one years old.

Each year, tourists stop by to visit Billy the Kid's grave in Fort Sumner, New Mexico. The grave is protected by iron bars.

THE LEGEND OF BILLY THE KID

Why is Billy the Kid so well known? Unlike Jesse James, the Kid never robbed a bank. He never held up a train or blew up a safe. The gangs he ran with never made much money from their crimes. In fact, his life as an outlaw lasted only four short years.

It is true that the Kid was quick on the trigger. A good guess is that he killed nine men. That was not even close to a record for those violent times. John Wesley Hardin, a far less famous gunslinger, killed forty-four men.

The Billy the Kid most people think they know is mostly legend. The tall tales tell us that the Kid killed his first man to protect his mother's name. After that he is said to have spent his short life fighting bad men like Jimmy Dolan. In this romantic version, the Kid kills a man for each of his twenty-one years.

Dime novels about Billy the Kid contained made-up stories about the famous outlaw. The stories, along with the books and movies that followed, have helped keep the Kid's memory alive.

Books often describe him as a western Robin Hood. Why did he steal? Why, to help the poor, of course—or so the story goes.

How did such a legend get started? Its roots lie in stories about the Kid that were told while he was alive. After the Kid died, Pat Garrett "wrote" *The Authentic Life of Billy the Kid*. The book's real author was Ash Upson, a New Mexico postmaster. Upson made up many of the stories in the book.

The legend grew when dime novels borrowed freely from the Garrett-Upson book. After the dime

More than 100 years after the Kid's death, the movie *Young Guns*, starring Emilio Estevez as Billy the Kid, was a huge hit.

novels came the movies. Most films picture the Kid as an outlaw-hero. This Billy the Kid came to life again in *Pat Garrett and Billy the Kid,* a 1973 movie. The popular film *Young Guns* followed in 1988. The History Channel tried to set the record straight in a 2007 program called *Investigating History: Billy the Kid.*

When it comes to telling the Kid's story, western writers still disagree. All of us, though, can agree on one thing. The legend of Billy the Kid will never be forgotten.

GLOSSARY

Apache Agency—A trading post for American Indians established by the U.S. government.

avenge—To get even with someone for a wrongdoing.

boarder—A guest who pays for a room and meals in a private home.

Code of the West—The unwritten rules men and women tried to live by in the Wild West.

constable—A law officer who keeps the peace in a town or village.

dime novels—Low-cost magazines that printed popular fiction during the late 1800s.

famine—A time when food is scarce and people starve.

foreman—The man or woman who directs the efforts of a work crew.

grand jury—A jury that has the job of deciding whether or not a suspect should stand trial for a crime.

gunslinger—Outlaws and lawmen of the Wild West who settled arguments with their guns.

indicted—To be charged with a crime.

jury—A group of citizens sworn to judge the facts and reach a decision in a legal matter.

justice of the peace (JP)—A lower-court official who hears minor cases. JPs also have the power to send cases to the higher courts and to marry people.

legend—A story that many people believe but which is almost always untrue.

pardon—A legal document that forgives someone for crimes he or she may have committed.

posse—A group of citizens who join with law enforcement officers to aid in the capture of outlaws.

Regulators—The name given to the gunslingers who supported Tunstall and McSween in the Lincoln County war.

rustler—Someone who steals horses or cattle.

scaffold—The platform on which a convicted criminal is hanged.

sombrero—A Spanish name for a wide-brimmed hat often worn in the Southwest and in Mexico.

FURTHER READING

Books

Airy, Helen. *Whatever Happened to Billy the Kid?* Santa Fe, N.M.: Sunstone Press, 2005.

Brothers, Mary Hudson and Bell Hudson. *Billy the Kid: The Most Hated, the Most Loved Outlaw New Mexico Ever Produced.* Whitefish, Mont.: Kessinger Publishing, 2007.

Garrett, Pat F. *The Authentic Life of Billy the Kid.* Santa Fe, N.M.: Sunstone Press, 2007.

Healy, Nick. *Billy the Kid.* Mankato, Minn.: Creative Education, 2005.

Johnson, Jim. *Billy the Kid: His Real Name Was ….* Parker, Colo.: Outskirts Press, 2006.

Landau, Elaine. *Billy the Kid: Wild West Outlaw.* Berkeley Heights, N.J.: Enslow, 2004.

Internet Addresses

About Billy the Kid
　http://www.aboutbillythekid.com/

EyeWitness to History.com: The Death of Billy the Kid, 1881
　http://www.eyewitnesstohistory.com/billythekid.htm

INDEX